6/06

MICHAEL GRAVES

MICHAEL GRAVES

IMAGES OF A GRAND TOUR

BRIAN M. AMBROZIAK

WITH A FOREWORD BY MICHAEL GRAVES

PRINCETON ARCHITECTURAL PRESS, NEW YORK

PUBLISHED BY
PRINCETON ARCHITECTURAL PRESS
37 EAST SEVENTH STREET
NEW YORK, NEW YORK 10003

FOR A FREE CATALOG OF BOOKS, CALL 1.800.722.6657.
VISIT OUR WEB SITE AT WWW.PAPRESS.COM.

EDITING: CLARE JACOBSON
ED. ASSISTANCE: JOHN MCGILL, LAUREN NELSON, AND DOROTHY BALL
DESIGN: SARA E. STEMEN

SPECIAL THANKS TO:
NETTIE ALJIAN, NICOLA BEDNAREK, JANET BEHNING, MEGAN CAREY,
PENNY (YUEN PIK) CHU, RUSSELL FERNANDEZ, JAN HAUX, JOHN
KING, MARK LAMSTER, NANCY EKLUND LATER, LINDA LEE, KATHARINE
MYERS, JANE SHEINMAN, SCOTT TENNENT, JENNIFER THOMPSON,
PAUL G. WAGNER, JOSEPH WESTON, AND DEB WOOD OF PRINCETON
ARCHITECTURAL PRESS
                    —KEVIN C. LIPPERT, PUBLISHER

LIBRARY OF CONGRESS CATALOGING-IN-PUBLICATION DATA

AMBROZIAK, BRIAN M. (BRIAN MICHAEL), 1970–
   MICHAEL GRAVES : IMAGES OF A GRAND TOUR / BRIAN M.
AMBROZIAK ; WITH A FOREWORD BY MICHAEL GRAVES.
     P. CM.
   INCLUDES BIBLIOGRAPHICAL REFERENCES.
   ISBN 1-56898-529-0 (PERMANENT PAPER)
   1. GRAVES, MICHAEL, 1934—NOTEBOOKS, SKETCHBOOKS, ETC.
   2. ARCHITECTURAL DRAWING—UNITED STATES—20TH CENTURY.
   3. GRAVES, MICHAEL, 1934 –TRAVEL—EUROPE. 4. ARCHITECTURE-
EUROPE-PICTORIAL WORKS. I. GRAVES, MICHAEL, 1934– II. TITLE.
   NA2707.G7A88 2005
   720 .92–DC22

CREDITS
*All images courtesy of Michael Graves
   except for the following:*
3L: Dublin City Gallery The Hugh
   Lane
4, 252, 253: Courtesy of Michael Graves
   & Associates
6: Städelsches Kunstinstitut, Frankfurt
   am Main
7L: By courtesy of the Trustees of
   Sir John Soane's Museum
7R: Bildarchiv Preussischer
   Kulturbesitz / Art Resource, NY
8T: © 2004 Artist Rights Society (ARS),
   New York / ADAGP, Paris / FLC
8B: Courtesy of the Pennsylvania
   Academy of the Fine Arts,
   Philadelphia. Gift of Mrs. Louis I.
   Kahn
10T: Photo courtesy of the Allan Stone
   Gallery, New York City
248B: Daniel Aubry, NYC
250: Stiftung Weimarer Klassik und
   Kunstsammlungen / Museen

Per il nostro insegnante,
Michael

CONTENTS

Michael Graves's room at the American Academy in Rome, Studio no. 9

FOREWORD

Michael Graves

THE EXTRAORDINARY EXPERIENCE of two years at the American Academy in Rome in the early 1960s transformed how I looked at the world around me. In that rich and marvelous city, I came to understand architecture as a continuum from antiquity to the present day, and thus as a language. I discovered new ways of seeing and analyzing both architecture and landscape. I also developed an urgent need to record what I saw and created hundreds of photographs and drawings. It has been a great joy to work with Brian Ambroziak on his ambitious project to publish many of them in this book, accompanied by his insightful commentary.

I have always been fascinated by drawing. In fact, it was my ability to draw that led me to a career in architecture. Until I went to Rome, however, I had created drawings only in my studio, never in the street or landscape. While there, rather than searching for a single manner of drawing, I experimented with multiple methods that I thought might express the architecture. I made large, elaborate sepia and black ink washes of important baroque churches, 40 x 28 inches in size; quick notations in fine ink or crude pencil in a hand-sized notebook; and pencil sketches on a wonderful cream-colored clay-coated paper, with fluid lines that captured just the essence of a profile. No matter what media I chose, my drawings were always analytical. It was important to me to reveal some salient characteristic of the architecture, perhaps its frontality, the layering of a spatial sequence, or simply the quality of a surface as it catches the light. I thought that if any one of my drawings were viewed as a travel scene, I had failed, since it would be merely picturesque.

While I was teaching and practicing architecture after my return from Rome, drawing became fundamental to my thought process. My 1977 article, "The Necessity for Drawing: Tangible Speculation," reprinted in this volume, describes the essential roles drawings play in creativity. When one draws, there is an intrinsic reciprocity between mind and act. Through their mnemonic qualities, drawings fix in our conscience what we have seen. By their fragmentary nature, they are inherently speculative and therefore contribute to the very conception of architecture.

ACKNOWLEDGMENTS

I FIRST MET MICHAEL GRAVES in 1996 in a design studio at Princeton University. Like hundreds of students before me, I was captivated by Michael's insightful use of history and his ability to convey his mental visual library through drawing. After graduating I continued my studies under Michael at his Princeton architectural office. There I saw firsthand the education of the architect. I observed a designer constantly looking through architecture, literally rubbing his hands across the pages of texts and committing the architectural images to memory. I saw an architect working at his desk, with the sound of the Reds or the Pacers playing on the radio, drawing into the late hours of the night after everyone else had left the office. And I was around an individual who cherished his role as that of teacher and friend. It was in this environment, one in which I desired to know even more about Michael, that I came across this collection of drawings and photographs from his stay at the American Academy in Rome. I will always be indebted to Michael for his support of this project, his confidence in me, and most importantly for granting me the opportunity to study these drawings and photographs that provide personal glimpses into the mind of Michael Graves: the architect, the artist, and the teacher.

While history tends to remember the individual, it is important to understand, especially in a field as complex and demanding as architecture, that there is a surrounding cast whose talents and ideas not only complement but give new direction to the vision of an architectural office. One such person is Karen Nichols, without whom this book would not have been possible. Her valuable insight as well as her passion for the firm and its vision had a constructive effect on the final product. I am especially thankful to Patrick Burke and Gary Lapera who, as design partners, allowed me to observe and participate daily in design decisions and take part in the daunting task of moving from paper to building. Courtney Havran, Marek Bulaj, Debbi Miller, and Caroline Hancock provided much appreciated help in tracking down images, articles, and permissions. As well, I appreciate the numerous other individuals at the office with whom I worked closely.

Support from the University of Tennessee has been invaluable in realizing the completion of this project. It has been a privilege to be surrounded by top scholars who have been most willing to provide advice and encouragement for this project. I owe a special thanks to the exceptional students at the university, especially those who traveled to Rome with me this past summer, whose enthusiasm and thoughtfulness make teaching and research a pleasure.

I would like to thank the Graham Foundation for their generous support of this project from the beginning. As well, I am grateful to the American Academy in Rome, who afforded me the chance to work as a Visiting Artist and see firsthand all that life at the academy has to offer. A special thanks goes to Director Lester Little, Assistant Director for Operations Pina Pasquantonio, and the American Academy in Rome Librarian Christina Huemer. I appreciate the support of Princeton Architectural Press, specifically, Clare Jacobson who continues to amaze me with her attention to detail and the care she devotes to each project.

Finally, I have to thank my wife Katherine without whom I could not have completed this project. Katherine was fortunate enough to have also studied under Michael in school and in practice and acquired a similar reverence for him as a teacher, an architect, and a friend. Her valuable insight, her willingness to review and edit material, and the exhausting pace that she set through streets of Rome were essential to defining the scope and content of this book.

Let me put it like this. In this place, whoever looks seriously about him and has eyes to see is bound to become a stronger character: he acquires a sense of strength hitherto unknown to him.
—JOHANN WOLFGANG VON GOETHE, FROM *Italian Journey*

Photograph of Michael Graves
drawing in the streets of Rome,
1961

THE NECESSITY FOR SEEING

IN 1960 MICHAEL GRAVES WAS AWARDED the American Academy in Rome's prestigious Prix de Rome. Having just completed his graduate studies in architecture, he embarked on a Grand Tour that led to a lifelong fascination with the landscape, the culture, and the history of Italy. During his time in Rome, Graves participated in daily social rituals that had been rehearsed for hundreds of years. Meals of pasta, cheese, and Chianti around simple wooden country tables bathed in the light of Tuscany revealed to him humanistic and domestic connections between the architecture and the landscape, the sacred and the profane. He learned that certain picturesque hillsides covered with umbrella pines and poplars were not natural landscapes, but rather had been meticulously designed and cultivated by a single Italian family over centuries. Through these examples he was exposed to ideas about architecture that went well beyond his modernist upbringing. His drawings and photographs from this time focus on the connection between the architecture and the land of Italy itself—"wistful, luminous, plain, its grain and olive trees, the stones of its buildings in prodigal light."[1] Graves learned through recording his journeys, discussing what he saw with fellow travelers and scholars, and participating in Italian customs, how architecture and landscape affect our perception and connection to the richness of our surroundings, and how an architect may draw upon these lessons to develop his or her own personal design.

The sketches and photographs of Italy that Graves produced during this two-year period visually imprinted themselves on his mind. The impact of his experiences is revealed throughout the extensive body of his work, a resume that encompasses painting, graphic design, and industrial design, and an architectural portfolio that ranges from pavilions to city plans. Graves's drawings, paintings, and photographs illustrate the architect's process, the means of translating experiences into design. In looking through this collection of impressions we see glimpses into the mind of one of the most significant and influential architects of the twentieth century.

*

LIKE MANY ARCHITECTS BEFORE HIM, Graves traveled to Italy to further his education. "No one who has not been here can have any conception of what an education in Rome is," Goethe wrote. "One is, so to speak, reborn and one's former ideas seem like a child's swaddling clothes. Here the most ordinary person becomes somebody, for his mind is enormously enlarged even if his character remains unchanged."[2] B. T. Leslie writes, "At a time in the 1960's when, under the flag of modernism, it was fashionable to reject the cultural traditions of Western Europe, Graves came to the American Academy in Rome to study the forms and language of architecture on the Italian peninsula."[3] His home there for two years was the American Academy in Rome, established on the highest point in the city, in and around the grounds of the Villa Aurelia. In the collegiate quarters of the academy, artists and scholars come together for meals under the arcade of an open courtyard, they work side by side in the library, and they converse during strolls through the gardens and in the streets of the surrounding neighborhoods. During his stay Graves was surrounded by top scholars working in archaeology, architecture, classical studies, design arts, historic preservation, art history, landscape architecture, literature, modern Italian studies, musical composition, postclassical humanistic studies, and the visual arts.

Graves benefited greatly from discussions with other fellows. One such person was the artist in residence Lennart Anderson, who commented to Graves that the large pen and ink washes he was making were not allowing him to see the building while he drew. (The photograph that appears at the beginning of this text captures Graves working on the cobblestone paving over one of these drawings, which measured several feet. Many of his pen and ink images were sold to fortunate passers-by to fund Graves's travels.)

Anderson also observed that by working on the ground, Graves was not establishing a vertical relationship to his subjects. These comments led Graves to begin working in a smaller format and to develop a reductive technique that used line sparingly in an attempt to capture the essence of what was being viewed.

Graves explored his new city and learned to understand it as a superimposition, one that layered the plan of Giambattista Nolli, the city scenes of Giuseppe Vasi and Giovanni Battista Piranesi, and the emotional qualities of light and the passage of time of the paintings of Jean-Baptiste-Camille Corot and of Giorgio de

LEFT: *Jean-Baptiste-Camille Corot,* Fountain of the French Academy, Rome, *1826–27, oil on canvas* RIGHT: *Michael Graves,* View from the Pincio, Rome, Italy, *1962, pencil sketch*

Chirico. He grew to appreciate the potential for architecture to communicate as a result of his tours.

Graves's nights were spent in the academy library looking through books, taking longhand notes prior to photocopiers, and planning excursions. He read through guidebooks that described Italy's major monuments and paged through volumes of drawings and paintings. Through this process he observed Rome through a historic and critical eye, to see what those before him had viewed as important. His daytime drawings show the influence of the images he observed in books during these late nights. Quite often, Graves positioned himself in a specific spot in order to draw or photograph through the eyes of a previous architect or artist. This process allowed him to compare the reality of significant sites to that of their representations. In both observing the site and studying its image, Graves joined the effort of architects before him to develop arguments based in history and culture. He has often commented that representation is seeing something anew. Through drawings, an architect captures the essence of an artifact, seeing it as a reoccurrence or a replica of a greater idea.

While one might look for direct connections between an architect's drawings and his built work, these literal one-to-one associations tend to be forced. It is more often the case that Graves draws from a multitude of experiences and transforms and

*Objects from the Grand Tour,
inkwells depicting the Temple of
Vesta, displayed in Graves's
personal library*

shapes them throughout his design process. When recalling these images, he claims he is not "treating or employing history, but rather participating in its continuities."[4]

In studying Italy's history, culture, and architecture, Graves began to question the unconditional nature of his modernist training. He had analyzed the work of Mies van der Rohe as an undergraduate at the University of Cincinnati and had become a disciple of Le Corbusier while a graduate student at Harvard. At the American Academy, Graves began to appreciate the continuum of history and to expand his architectural vocabulary. The drawings and photographs from this period are not mere diaries; they are designs in that they are critical investigations, yielding a new way of thinking about architecture. In studying these images we not only retrace Graves's steps but discover new things about the development of the architect's discourse, a synthesis of what he saw and what architects before him had drawn.

While Graves spent the majority of his time abroad in Rome, he did take several trips to see other parts of Italy and Europe. The pace on these trips was relaxed; Graves would drive to a site, set up camp, photograph and draw, and then pick up and go to the next site. Camping for twenty-five cents a night allowed him the luxury of keeping his schedule flexible. Typically, he drove between twenty to one hundred miles a day, with a maximum of three hundred miles. His first trip took Graves by boat to the Greek island of Mykonos, and then to Athens, up through Bulgaria, and to Istanbul to see the mosques and the city. From there, he traveled through Yugoslavia, up the Adriatic Coast, and back to Italy. He saw Venice and Ravenna for the first time on this trip and then traveled back to Rome. Other trips took him to Spain, England, Germany, and France, where he saw most everything Le Corbusier had built at that time.

THE IDEA OF TRAVEL AS A MEANS OF ENLIGHTENMENT goes back as far as the second century when Pope Gregory, upon seeing fair haired boys in the Roman marketplace, remarked, "Non Angli, sed Angeli," and vowed to convert the English to Christianity. In the centuries that followed countless faithful followed the Pilgrim's Way across the Chalk Downs to the English Channel, and traversed Merovingian, Carolingian, Bourbon France, and the long roads of Italy until they came to Roma Sacra.[5] Centuries later, the purpose of travel abroad extended beyond spiritual enlightenment as young gentlemen set out to enhance their formal education, to see

Johann Heinrich Wilhelm Tischbein, Goethe in the Roman Campagna, *1787, oil on canvas*

the art and architecture of classic lands, and to expand their understanding of foreign etiquette, traditions, and government.

In 1670 the phrase "Grand Tour" first appeared in the preface of Richard Lassels's *The Voyage of Italy*. By the eighteenth century the Grand Tour, which often lasted from a few months to several years, had become part of the expected education of every European nobleman, and then every student of architecture.[6] The primary destination of this Tour was Italy, with its heritage of ancient Roman monuments and picturesque landscapes. "The man who has not been to Italy," wrote Samuel Johnson, "is always conscious of an inferiority from his not having seen what is expected a man should see."[7]

The lessons of the Grand Tour were more personalized by Sir John Soane than probably any other eighteenth-century British architect.[8] In 1776 Soane was awarded

LEFT: *Henry Parke*, Sir John Soane Royal Academy Lecture Drawing, View of a Student on a Ladder, with Rod, Measuring the Corinthian Order, Temple of Castor and Pollux (Temple of Jupiter Stator), Rome, *circa 1814–20, pencil, pen, and watercolor* RIGHT: *Karl Friedrich Schinkel*, On the Top of Mount Aetna at Sunrise, *1804, Pen and ink and wash on paper*

a traveling fellowship by the Royal Institute of British Architects. During his twenty-seven month voyage through Italy, he created and compiled hundreds of drawings and paintings that would later serve as the foundation for his Royal Academy lectures. The collection primarily contains archaeological records and includes measured drawings, sketches, and comparative illustrations that detail issues of proportion and scale.[9]

Another important figure of the eighteenth-century Grand Tour is the German architect Karl Friedrich Schinkel. Schinkel's architecture responded to the classical forms of the Mediterranean that he observed and sketched on his travels throughout Italy. To supplement his accurate sketching, Schinkel developed a series of historical re-creations, inventive paintings possessing a strong narrative quality. He used the drawings and paintings from his travels to investigate the relationship

Le Corbusier, Sketches of
Michelangelo's Campidoglio,
1911, pencil sketch

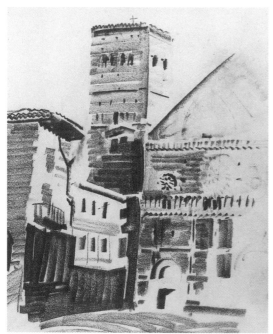

Louis I. Kahn, Assisi, *Italy,
1929, graphite on thin ivory
paper*

between space and vision, a topic that would consume his career and define his architecture.[10] The American architect Julia Morgan, the first woman admitted into the architectural program at the prestigious Ecole des Beaux-Arts in 1898, not only studied Paris but took several trips around Europe, visiting sites and sketching her impressions.[11]

Italy continued to play an important role in the education of the architect into the twentieth century. Even when photography replaced drawing as the primary method for producing images, architects still chose to draw in order to better impress the physical reality of a scene into their memories. The Swedish architect Erik Gunnar Asplund returned home from his journey through Italy with hundreds of postcards of architecture, paintings, and sculpture to supplement more than three hundred pages of drawings, sketches, annotations, and portraits.[12] Le Corbusier carried a camera with him on his earliest voyage to Rome in 1911, yet relied most heavily on the sketch to record the image.[13] He stated, "When one travels and works with visual things . . . one uses one's eyes and draws, so as to fix deep down in one's experience what is seen. . . . All this means first to look, and then to observe, and finally to discover. Once the impression has been recorded by the pencil, it stays for good, entered, registered, inscribed."[14] The architect Louis Kahn claims to have found himself architecturally during his sketching trips through Italy. Kahn captured what he called the "little village" of Italian medieval and vernacular architecture in a series of graphite drawings and watercolors.[15]

Graves could certainly relate to Kahn's sentiments. While many of his drawings and photographs show the quintessential monuments and architectural masterpieces of Italy, a great deal pay attention to humble, nondescript vernacular architecture or anonymous corners of ruins that suggest not history but the passage of time.

THROUGHOUT HIS LIFE, GRAVES HAS MAINTAINED an interest in drawing and painting, a passion that he developed as a young child. He often tells the story of how his mother advised him that being an artist was an extremely difficult way to earn a living. When he asked her what the other options might be, she suggested that he consider engineering or architecture. After hearing what an engineer did, he decided to become an architect.

And so it makes good sense that Graves spent much of his architectural fellowship pursuing the artistic representation of buildings. Graves focused on three media

Willem de Kooning,
Black and White Rome,
*1959, oil on paper on
canvas*

FAR LEFT: *Michael
Graves,* Composition,
1961, pen and ink wash

LEFT: *Michael Graves,*
Composition, *1961, pen
and ink wash*

BELOW: *Michael Graves,*
Composition, *1961,
oil on canvas*

in his work: pencil sketches, pen and ink drawings, and photographs. Each in its own way brought him to an understanding of his subject.

Pencil and paper are investigative tools quite different from the camera. Often what architects choose not to draw is as important as what they choose to draw. Graves rarely focused on details but instead portrayed the massiveness of structures through their abstraction. He used line sparingly to delineate a carefully constructed composition, sporadically to express sculptural movement, or boldly to define shadow in mass or a tonal field.

The idea of the drawing as a tool for investigation is quite apparent in many of Graves's shorthand sketches. This method of drawing, similar to Le Corbusier's and patterned after the speed of the camera, reduced the image to essential lines. Quick studies allowed Graves to portray different aspects of the same site. For example, the drawings of Carcassonne provide a study of a varied perceptual experience. The fortified medieval town is portrayed from the distance, from within the winding medieval streets, and from the air (pages 188–191). This sequence is illustrated in many of Graves's architectural designs. Breaking up a site into different scales so that an inhabitant might better find his place is critical to Graves's way of thinking about architecture.

The ink wash technique Graves used relies heavily on his paintings from this period, which were very much influenced by the work of Willem de Kooning and other American Abstract Expressionists. In de Kooning's *Black and White Rome* (1959), the gestural technique yields an image in which form becomes secondary to the impulses of the artist. An obvious connection exists between this work and Graves's *Compositions*, completed early in his first year at the Academy. Graves also drew from the work of the Italian "Art Informale" painters, whose work was being shown around Rome at the time. The drawings by these artists were created spontaneously and at rapid speed so as to give voice to the subconscious of the artist.

In Graves's pen and ink drawings, one sees the same frenzied pace in the application of line work. However, the abstraction that occurs in these drawings does not occur over the entire subject but only in localized moments. These drawings clearly depict their subject matter and introduce an implied light source through the spacing of lines and the build-up of ink. Many of the drawings include ink washes that range from transparent grays to pitch black, implying depth and a sense of hierarchy on the

Michael Graves, Window with
Balcony, *Rome, Italy, 1961,
Kodachrome slide*

page. They include very little negative space and create a sense of compression as they push to the edges of the paper.

While Graves recorded his Grand Tour extensively through his drawing, he also turned to photography as a means of documenting what he saw. Many of the photographs share scenes with his sketchbooks, but Graves primarily used the camera to capture aspects of the architecture and the landscape that were more readily expressed by the quick shot than by pencil or ink. The photographs tend to focus on issues of detail, color, texture, and light. Each creates a composition whose physical content, while beautiful in its own right, is framed in such a way as to express an underlying theme. It is this investigation that allows Graves to transcend stylistic issues and focus on revealing a language that will later provide the words for his architecture.

Shadow is a critical element in Graves's photographs. It is incorporated almost as if it were another material in his palette. The quality of the crisp Mediterranean light, heightened by the warm colors of Italian buildings, yields an effect that is seen in few places in the world. Graves's photographs focus on this effect. Color and detail are two elements that would be difficult to describe through a quick field sketch but are ideally suited for a photograph. As an architect who continually paints, Graves is extremely sensitive to color, and his study through photography has enabled him to develop a palette that recalls the colors of Roman architecture and its landscape. The warm muted tones of Graves's architecture—blues that range from a bright sky to a deep shadow and greens that evoke natural materials such as copper—appear repeatedly in his photographs.

LOCATED ON THE GROUND FLOOR of Graves's Princeton office is a small room whose walls are filled with trays of slides. Graves has returned to Italy repeatedly throughout his career to continue on the path of inquiry that he started in 1960. This slide room includes thousands of images from his travels, architectural precedents, and records of his own design work. It is common to see Graves bent over the light table with a magnifier studying these slides, just as he leafs through the sketchbooks in his library. The travel photographs and sketches that he views recall distinct memories and capture conditions that activate his senses. These catalogued moments inform his architecture, his product design, and his writings.

In looking at Graves's travel drawings and photographs from his Grand Tour, we must understand them not as mere postcards that mark destinations. Rather, they are composed to imprint upon the architect's mind a central idea about culture and history to remember and assimilate. This idea, portrayed through a range of graphic techniques, follows an acute awareness of the methods employed by architects and artists throughout history. Graves recalls and combines these representations to create detailed compositions that convey new meaning. The drawings and photographs contained in this book provide the key to understanding Graves's intentions as an architect—one who participates in the continuity of history and draws freely from a memory engraved by examples of modern and premodern architectural precedent. As such, they record the education of an architect, exploring his struggle to reveal himself on paper. The drawings and photographs of Michael Graves transcend formal analysis and through color, shadow, and line capture an essence that is Italy.

1. Paul F. Kirby, *The Grand Tour in Italy: 1700–1800* (New York: S. F. Vanni, 1952), xiii.

2. Johann Wolfgang von Goethe, *Italian Journey*, trans. W. H. Auden and Elizabeth Mayer (London: Penguin, 1952), 150.

3. B. T. Leslie, "The Gestalt of Graves," *Michael Graves: Idee e projetti 1981–1991* (Milan: Electa, 1991), 43.

4. Alex Buck and Matthias Vogt, eds., *Michael Graves: Designer Monographs 3* (New York: St. Martin's Press, 1994), 68.

5. Kirby, *Grand Tour*, 2.

6. Ibid.

7. James Boswell, *Life of Johnson*, ed. R. W. Chapman (1904; repr., Oxford: Oxford University Press, 1998), 742.

8. David Watkin, "Sir John Soane's Grand Tour: Its Impact on His Architecture and His Collections," in Clare Hornsby, ed., *The Impact of Italy: The Grand Tour and Beyond* (London: British School at Rome, 2000), 101–119.

9. Like Soane, Graves is an avid collector. His residence in Princeton, New Jersey, provides a landscape for placing works of art that include a collection of Greek, Roman, and Etruscan vases, 17th- and 18th-century engravings, rare architectural drawings, and several pristine pieces of Biedermeier furniture. As in Soane's house, these objects represent memories and contain ideas that Graves reflects upon and expands daily in his life and his architecture.

10. Barry Bergdoll, *Karl Friedrich Schinkel: An Architecture for Prussia* (New York: Rizzoli International, 1994), 24.

11. Sara Holmes Boutella, *Julia Morgan: Architect* (New York: Abbeville Press Publishers, 1995), 33.

12. Luca Ortelli, "Heading South: Asplund's Impressions," *Lotus International* 68 (1991): 22–33.

13. See Le Corbusier, *Voyage d'Orient: Sketchbooks* (New York: Rizzoli, 1988) for an exceptionally accurate reproduction of the architect's sketchbooks, including his drawings and notes.

14. Le Corbusier, *Creation is a Patient Search*, trans. J. Palmes (New York: Praeger, 1960), 37.

15. For a description of sketching abroad and a comprehensive collection of Louis Kahn's travel sketches, see Eugene Johnson and Michael J. Lewis, *Drawn From the Source: The Travel Sketches of Louis I. Kahn* (Cambridge: MIT Press, 1996), 34.

PLATES

The drawings and photographs that follow are grouped by location. Images in Rome are organized by ten general neighborhoods, including the Janiculum Hill where the American Academy in Rome is located; the Imperial Forums that include the buildings, monuments, and ruins along the Via dei Fori Imperiali; the Capitoline Hill leading down to the banks of the Tiber River; the Palatine Hill; Campo Marzio; Vatican City; Tridente defined by the Via del Corso, Via di Ripetta, and Via del Babuino, leading up to the Pincio Hill; Quirinale; the Caelian Hill including the surrounding valleys; and areas outside of Rome including the Appian Way. Sites in the section entitled "Other Italian Locales" are grouped by regions, while European destinations are by country.

SANTA MARIA MADDALENA
Campo Marzio, Rome, Italy
Date unknown
Pen drawing

ROME

left

TEMPIETTO
DEL BRAMANTE
Janiculum Hill, Rome, Italy
May 18, 1961
Pen drawing

opposite

FONTANA
DELL'ACQUA PAOLA
Janiculum Hill, Rome, Italy
May 30, 1961
Pen and ink wash

FLAVIAN AMPHITHEATRE,
COLOSSEUM, NOS. 1 AND 2
Imperial Forums, Rome, Italy
1961
Kodachrome slide

"ROMA"
Imperial Forums, Rome, Italy
October 1961
Pen and ink wash

"ROME FROM MY STUDIO"
Janiculum Hill, Rome, Italy
November 26, 1961
Pencil sketch

above

ARCH OF CONSTANTINE
Imperial Forums, Rome, Italy
Date unknown
Pen and ink wash

opposite

ARCH OF CONSTANTINE, OBLIQUE
Imperial Forums, Rome, Italy
Date unknown
Pen and ink wash

"BASILICA OF
MAXENTIUS"
*Imperial Forums,
Rome, Italy
1960
Pen and ink wash*

ARCH OF SEPTIMIUS SEVERUS, NOS. 1 AND 2

Imperial Forums, Rome, Italy

1961

Kodachrome slide

ROMAN FORUM
Imperial Forums, Rome, Italy
Date unknown
Kodachrome slide

"SANTA MARIA DI LORETO, ROME"
Imperial Forums, Rome, Italy
July 4, 1961
Pen and ink wash

"SANTI NOME DI MARIA, ROME"
Imperial Forums, Rome, Italy
1961
Pen and ink wash

S. Nome di Maria, Roma
Richard Gavris 1984

SAN LUCA E SANTA MARTINA
Imperial Forums, Rome, Italy
Date unknown
Pen and ink wash

SAN LUCA E SANTA MARTINA, CUPOLA
Imperial Forums, Rome, Italy
1960
Pen and ink wash

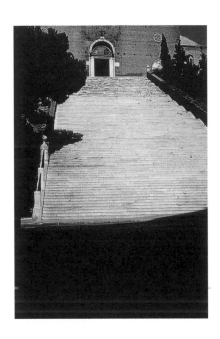

SANTA MARIA IN ARACOELI, NO. 1
Capitoline Hill, Rome, Italy
1962
Kodachrome slide

SANTA MARIA IN ARACOELI, NO. 2
Capitoline Hill, Rome, Italy
Date illegible
Pen drawing

opposite
SANTA MARIA IN ARACOELI, NO. 3
Capitoline Hill, Rome, Italy
Date unknown
Pencil sketch

PALAZZO SENATORIO
Capitoline Hill, Rome, Italy
May 26, 1961
Pen and ink wash

BOCCA DELLA VERITA
(MOUTH OF TRUTH)
Capitoline Hill, Rome, Italy
Date unknown
Pen and ink wash

"SANTA MARIA IN COSMEDIN, ROME"
Capitoline Hill, Rome, Italy
October 1961
Pencil sketch

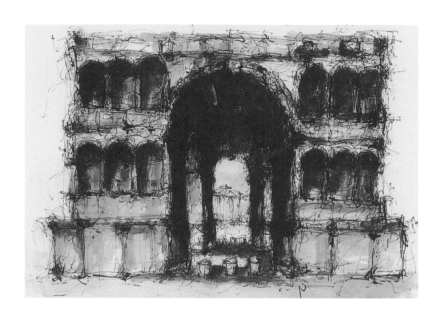

top
ARCH OF JANUS FRAMING
TEMPLE OF VESTA
Capitoline Hill, Rome, Italy
Date unknown
Pen and ink wash

bottom
ARCH OF JANUS AND
TEMPLE OF VESTA
Capitoline Hill, Rome, Italy
Date unknown
Pencil sketch

SANT'ANASTASIA AND DOMUS AUGUSTANA
Palatine Hill, Rome, Italy
Date unknown
Pencil sketch

opposite

"DOMUS AUGUSTANA, ROME"
Palatine Hill, Rome, Italy
1961
Pen and ink wash

above

PIAZZA NAVONA, SANT'AGNESE
IN AGONE
Campo Marzio, Rome, Italy
May 21, 1961
Pen and ink wash

SANT'IVO ALLA SAPIENZA, NO. 1
Campo Marzio, Rome, Italy
May 17, 1961
Pen and ink wash

SANT'IVO ALLA SAPIENZA, NO. 2
Campo Marzio, Rome, Italy
July 14, 1961
Pen drawing

SANT'IVO ALLA SAPIENZA, PLAN
Campo Marzio, Rome, Italy
Date unknown
Pen and ink wash

SANT'AGOSTINO
Campo Marzio, Rome, Italy
Date unknown
Pen and ink wash

VIEW FROM THE PANTHEON DOME

Campo Marzio, Rome, Italy

1961

Kodachrome slide

OCULUS OF THE PANTHEON

Campo Marzio, Rome, Italy

1961

Kodachrome slide

top

PORTA SANTO SPIRITO
Vatican City, Rome, Italy
Date unknown
Pen and ink wash

bottom

PORTA SANTO SPIRITO,
NICHE DETAIL
Vatican City, Rome, Italy
1961
Kodachrome slide

above

PIAZZA SAN PIETRO, BERNINI'S COLONNADE
Vatican City, Rome, Italy
Date unknown
Pen and ink wash

right

PIAZZA SAN PIETRO, CARRIAGES
Vatican City, Rome, Italy
1962
Kodachrome slide

above

"SAN PIETRO, ROME"
Vatican City, Rome, Italy
April 27, 1962
Pencil sketch

right

SAN PIETRO,
BALDACCHINO
Vatican City, Rome, Italy
Date unknown
Pencil sketch

"MICHELANGELO'S DOME"
Vatican City, Rome, Italy
November 19, 1961
Pen drawing

opposite, top
"SAINT PETER'S, ROME"
Vatican City, Rome, Italy
1961
Pen and ink wash

SAN PIETRO, MICHELANGELO'S DOME
Vatican City, Rome, Italy
February 12, 1961
Pen and ink wash

opposite, bottom
VIEW OF THE DOME OF SAN PIETRO
FROM UNDER THE PONTE GARABALDI
Rome, Italy
1961
Kodachrome slide

Cortile della Pigna
Vaticano

opposite
"CORTILE DELLA
PIGNA, VATICAN"
Vatican City, Rome, Italy
April, 1962
Pencil sketch

above
SANTA MARIA DEI
MIRACOLI E SANTA MARIA
IN MONTESANTO
Tridente, Rome, Italy
Date unknown
Pencil sketch

right
"CHIGI CHAPEL IN
SANTA MARIA DEL
POPOLO, ROME"
Tridente, Rome, Italy
April 26, 1962
Pencil sketch

SPANISH STEPS

Tridente, Rome, Italy

1961

Kodachrome slide

SPANISH STEPS, TRINITÀ DEI MONTI

Tridente, Rome, Italy

1961

Kodachrome slide

The Pincio and the
Villa Medici
from the Spanish Steps
Edward Craven 1962

opposite
"THE PINCIO AND THE
VILLA MEDICI FROM
THE SPANISH STEPS"
Tridente, Rome, Italy
1962
Pencil sketch

above
GARDEN OF THE VILLA MEDICI
Tridente, Rome, Italy
Date unknown
Kodachrome slide

right
"ROME FROM THE PINCIO"
Tridente, Rome, Italy
1962
Pencil sketch

opposite

"SAN ANDREA DELLE FRATTE"
Tridente, Rome, Italy
1962
Pencil sketch

above

VILLA BORGHESE
Borghese Gardens, Rome, Italy
Date unknown
Pen and ink wash

"FONTANA DEL TRITONE"

Quirinale, Rome, Italy

January 1962

Pen drawing

"TRITONE FOUNTAIN, ROME"

Quirinale, Rome, Italy

September 1961

Pen and ink wash

FOUNTAIN, NO. 1

Rome, Italy

Date unknown

Pen and ink wash

FOUNTAIN, NO. 2

Rome, Italy

1960

Pen and ink wash

above

"SANTA MARIA
MAGGIORE, ROME"
Esquiline Hill, Rome, Italy
October 1961
Pen drawing

right

SANTA MARIA
MAGGIORE, APSE
Esquiline Hill, Rome, Italy
Date unknown
Pencil sketch

SAN MARCELLO AL CORSO
Tridente, Rome, Italy
1961
Kodachrome slide

opposite

PIAZZA DEL QUIRINALE,
STAIRS
Quirinale, Rome, Italy
1961
Kodachrome slide

right

"SAN CARLINO, ROME,"
NO. I
Quirinale, Rome, Italy
February 1962
Pencil sketch

left

SAN CARLINO
Quirinale, Rome, Italy
May 20, 1961
Pen and ink wash

opposite

"SAN CARLINO, ROME,"
NO. 2
Quirinale, Rome, Italy
May 20, 1961
Pen and ink wash

VIEW UP CIRCULAR STAIRWELL
Rome, Italy
Date unknown
Kodachrome slide

"SAN GIOVANNI IN LATERANO, ROME"
Caelian Hill, Rome, Italy
Date unknown
Pen and ink wash

opposite and above

SANTO STEFANO ROTONDO, INTERIOR, NOS. 1–4
Caelian Hill, Rome, Italy
Date unknown
Pencil sketch

opposite and above

SANTO STEFANO ROTONDO, INTERIOR, NOS. 5–7
Caelian Hill, Rome, Italy
Date unknown
Pencil sketch

"BATHS OF CARACALLA"
Caelian Hill, Rome, Italy
January 26, 1962
Pen drawing

BATHS OF CARACALLA, MOSAICS, NOS. 1–4
Caelian Hill, Rome, Italy
1961
Kodachrome slide

opposite

SANTA CROCE IN GERUSALEMME
East of Rome, Italy
Date unknown
Pen and ink wash

below

SANTA COSTANZA
East of Rome, Italy
Date unknown
Pen and ink wash

TEMPLE OF MINERVA
MEDICA, RUINS OF THE
NYMPHAEUM OF THE
GARDENS OF LICINIUS
East of Rome, Italy
1961
Kodachrome slide

TOMB OF EURYSACES
(THE BAKER'S TOMB)
East of Rome, Italy
1961
Kodachrome slide

top
"APPIA ANTICA"
Appian Way, Rome, Italy
1961
Pencil sketch

bottom
CIRCUS OF MAXENTIUS
Appian Way, Rome, Italy
1960
Kodachrome slide

"SOUTH OF ROME"
Rome, Italy
1961
Pencil sketch

WINDOW WITH SHUTTERS   WINDOW WITH BALCONY
Rome, Italy   *Rome, Italy*
1961   *1961*
Kodachrome slide   *Kodachrome slide*

THRESHOLD, NOS. 1 AND 2

Rome, Italy

1961

Kodachrome slide

OTHER
ITALIAN LOCALES

LAZIO

HADRIAN'S VILLA, RUINS
Tivoli, Italy
Date unknown
Pencil sketch

top
HADRIAN'S VILLA,
VAULT
Tivoli, Italy
1960
Kodachrome slide

bottom
HADRIAN'S VILLA,
THE GREEK LIBRARY
Tivoli, Italy
1960
Kodachrome slide

opposite

HADRIAN'S VILLA, ARCADE
Tivoli, Italy
1961
Kodachrome slide

above

TEMPLE OF VESTA
Tivoli, Italy
1961
Kodachrome slide

CATHEDRAL OF SANTA
MARIA, CAMPANILE
Anagni, Italy
1960
Kodachrome slide

"ANAGNI, CAMPANILE
OF THE DUOMO"
Anagni, Italy
1960
Pen and ink wash

SANTA ROSALINA
Palestrina, Italy
1961
Kodachrome slide

NICHE
Palestrina, Italy
Date unknown
Kodachrome slide

opposite
IL PIANO "DEGLI EMICICLI,"
TEMPIO DELLA FORTUNA
PRIMIGENIA
Palestrina, Italy
1962
Kodachrome slide

STEPS TO PALAZZO BARBERINI
Palestrina, Italy
1961
Kodachrome slide

CASTELLO
Ostia Nuova, Italy
1960
Kodachrome slide

top
RUINS
Ostia Antica, Italy
1961
Kodachrome slide

bottom
CORNICE
Ostia Antica, Italy
1961
Kodachrome slide

top

SQUARE OF THE CORPORATIONS,
DOLPHIN MOSAIC
Ostia Antica, Italy
1961
Kodachrome slide

bottom

SQUARE OF THE CORPORATIONS,
ELEPHANT MOSAIC
Ostia Antica, Italy
1961
Kodachrome slide

DOMUS INTERIOR, HEARTH
Ostia Antica, Italy
1962
Kodachrome slide

DOMUS DETAILS
Ostia Antica, Italy
1961
Kodachrome slide

above

WATER BASIN
Ostia Antica, Italy
1961
Kodachrome slide

opposite

ISOLA SACRA, NOS. 1 AND 2
Ostia Antica, Italy
1961
Kodachrome slide

"SUTRI"
Sutri, Italy
1960
Pen and ink wash

"VITERBO, DINTORNINI DE ROMA"

Viterbo, Italy

1961

Pen and ink wash

opposite

CRYPTOPORTICO
OF THE SANCTUARY OF
JUPITER ANXUR
Terracina, Italy
1961
Kodachrome slide

right

TOMB OF MARCUS
TULLIUS CICERO
Near Formia, Italy
1961
Kodachrome slide

Santa Maria delle Carceri, Prato
7/42 Graves

opposite

"SANTA MARIA DELLE
CARCERI, PRATO"
Prato, Italy
April 1962
Pencil sketch

above

"BRUNELLESCHI DOME, FLORENCE"
Florence, Italy
April 19, 1962
Pencil sketch

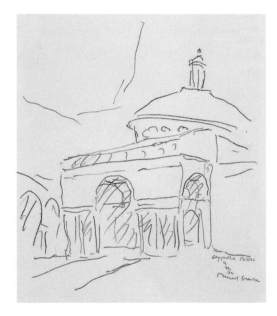

"PAZZI CHAPEL, FLORENCE"
Florence, Italy
April 20, 1962
Pencil sketch

"CAPPELLA PAZZI"
Florence, Italy
April 20, 1962
Pencil sketch

opposite
"MEDICI CHAPEL, FLORENCE"
Florence, Italy
April 1962
Pencil sketch

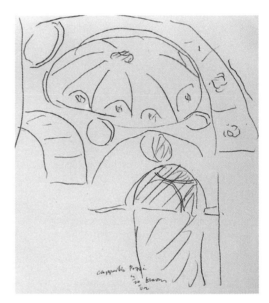

above and opposite

"CAPPELLA PAZZI," NOS. 3–6

Florence, Italy
April 20, 1962
Pencil sketch

SANTA MARIA NOVELLA, FACADE DETAIL
Florence, Italy
1961
Kodachrome slide

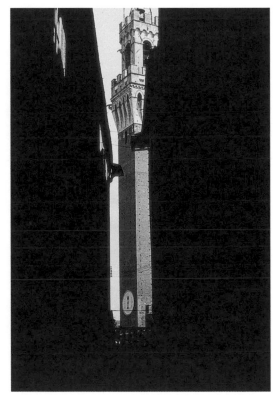

VIEW THROUGH ARCH
San Gimignano, Italy
1962
Kodachrome slide

VIEW OF TOWER
Siena, Italy
1961
Kodachrome slide

"SIENA, THE CAMPO," NOS. 1 AND 2

Siena, Italy

April 1962

Pencil sketch

"SIENA, THE BAPTISTRY OF THE DUOMO"

Siena, Italy

April 1962

Pencil sketch

"SIENA, THE DUOMO"

Siena, Italy

April 1962

Pencil sketch

PIEDMONT

"LA CAPPELLA
PORTINARI, MILANO"
Milan, Italy
April 16, 1962
Pencil sketch

above left

"FIRST CHAPEL ON THE RIGHT
IN THE BASILICA
DI S. EUSTORGIO, MILANO"
Milan, Italy
April 16, 1962
Pencil sketch

above right

"SANTA MARIA PRESSO, SAN
SATIRO, MILANO," NO. 1
Milan, Italy
April 16, 1962
Pencil sketch

right

"SANTA MARIA PRESSO, SAN
SATIRO, MILANO," NO. 2
Milan, Italy
April 17, 1962
Pencil sketch

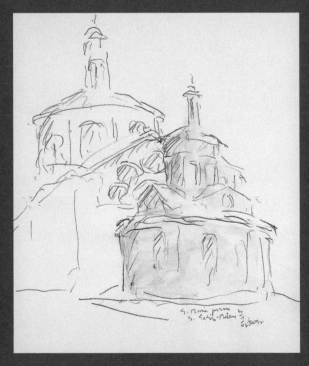

"SANTA MARIA DELLA
GRAZIE, MILANO,"
NOS. 1–3
Milan, Italy
April 1962
Pencil sketch

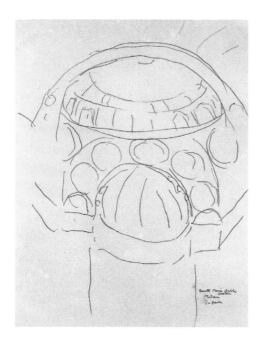

GALLERIA VITTORIO
EMANUELE, INTERIOR
DOME
Milan, Italy
Date unknown
Kodachrome slide

"THE GALLERIA, MILANO"
Milan, Italy
April 19, 1962
Pencil sketch

VENETO

"LA ROTONDA, VICENZA"
Vicenza, Italy
1961
Pencil sketch

SAN MARCO, VIEW FROM CANAL
Venice, Italy
November 5, 1961
Pencil sketch

SAN MARCO, FRAMED VIEW
FROM PIAZZA ARCADE
Venice, Italy
1962
Kodachrome slide

"SAN MARCO"
Venice, Italy
November 5, 1961
Pencil sketch

SAN MARCO, VIEW FROM
PIAZZA
Venice, Italy
November 5, 1961
Pencil sketch

San Marco Venezia
June '62
Michael Graves

"SAN MARCO, VENEZIA"
Venice, Italy
June 1962
Pencil sketch

SAN MARCO,
FACADE DETAIL
Venice, Italy
1961
Kodachrome slide

DOGE'S PALACE,
CORTILE, WITH DOMES
OF SAN MARCO
Venice, Italy
1961
Kodachrome slide

CA'D'ORO ON THE GRAND CANAL

Venice, Italy

1961

Kodachrome slide

SANTA MARIA DELLA SALUTE

Venice, Italy

Date unknown

Pen and ink wash

"RIMINI, MALATESTIANO,"
NOS. 1 AND 2
Rimini, Italy
April 1962
Pencil sketch

"RAVENNA, MAUSOLEO DI
GALLA PLACIDIA"
Ravenna, Italy
April 1962
Pencil sketch

"RAVENNA, SAN VITALE"
Ravenna, Italy
April 1962
Pencil sketch

DUOMO, COLUMN DETAIL

Modena, Italy

1962

Kodachrome slide

"MODENA, DUOMO," NO. 1

Modena, Italy

April 1962

Pencil sketch

"MODENA, DUOMO," NO. 2
Modena, Italy
April 1962
Pencil sketch

"PARMA, BATTISTERO,"
NOS. 1–3
Parma, Italy
April 1962
Pencil sketch

"URBINO, SAN BERNARDINO"
Urbino, Italy
April 1962
Pencil sketch

UMBRIA

CATHEDRAL DETAIL
Spoleto, Italy
1961
Kodachrome slide

"SAN FRANCESCO, ASSISI"
Assisi, Italy
April 8, 1962
Pencil sketch

DUOMO, NOS. 1 AND 2
Orvieto, Italy
1962
Kodachrome slide

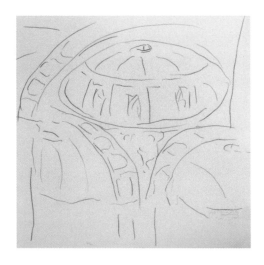

"SANTA MARIA DELLA CONSOLAZIONE,
TODI," NOS. 1–3
Todi, Italy
April 25, 1962
Pencil sketch

TRULLI HOUSES, ROOFS
Near Alberobello, Italy
Date unknown
Pen drawing

opposite
TRULLI HOUSES
Near Alberobello, Italy
Date unknown
Kodachrome slide

this page
TRULLI HOUSES, ROOF
DETAIL, NOS. 1 AND 2
Near Alberobello, Italy
1961
Kodachrome slide

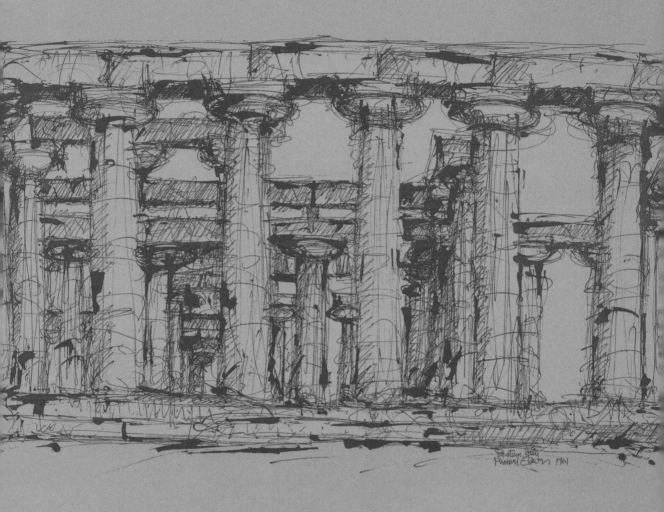

"PAESTUM, ITALY"
Paestum, Italy
1961
Pen drawing

WATER BASIN
Paestum, Italy
1961
Kodachrome slide

left
TEMPLE OF NEPTUNE,
TIERED COLUMNS
Paestum, Italy
1961
Kodachrome slide

opposite, top
TEMPLE OF NEPTUNE,
COLUMN BASE
Paestum, Italy
1961
Kodachrome slide

opposite, bottom
TEMPLE OF NEPTUNE,
PROFILE
Paestum, Italy
1961
Kodachrome slide

top
TEMPLE OF NEPTUNE,
COLUMNS
Paestum, Italy
1961
Kodachrome slide

bottom
TEMPLE OF NEPTUNE,
COLUMN FLUTING
Paestum, Italy
Date unknown
Kodachrome slide

opposite
TEMPLE OF NEPTUNE
Paestum, Italy
Date unknown
Kodachrome slide

TEMPLE OF NEPTUNE,
COLUMN FRAGMENTS,
NOS. 1 AND 2
Paestum, Italy
Date unknown
Kodachrome slide

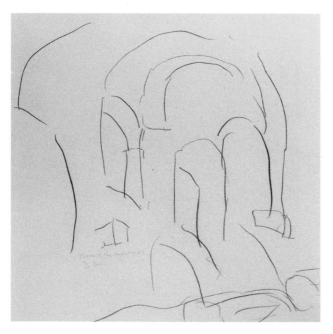

"POZZUOLI, THE
AMPHITHEATER,"
NOS. 2 AND 3
Pozzuoli, Italy
March 28, 1962
Pencil sketch

"BAY OF POZZUOLI"
Pozzuoli, Italy
March 28, 1962
Pencil sketch

Pompeii
the house

UNIDENTIFIED ITALIAN LOCALES

ARCADE
Location unknown, Italy
Date unknown
Kodachrome slide

ACROPOLIS, NO. 1
Athens, Greece
1961
Pencil sketch

GREECE

ACROPOLIS, NOS. 2 AND 3
Athens, Greece
1961
Pencil sketch

THEATER OF DIONYSIA
Athens, Greece
Date unknown
Pen drawing

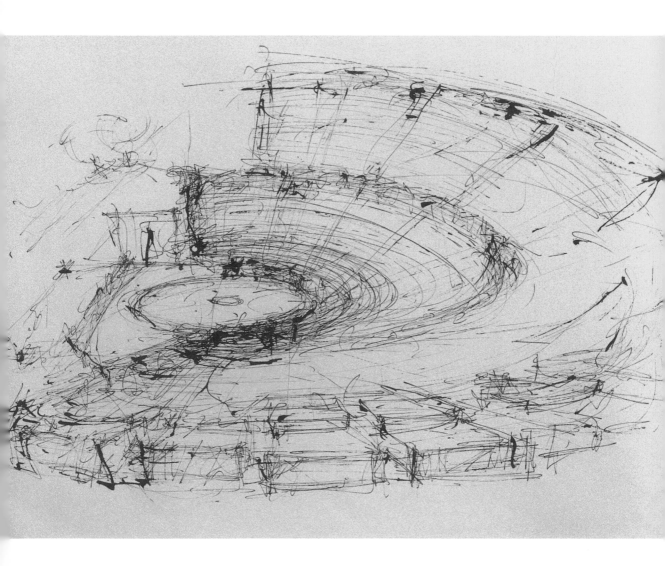

opposite, top

PARTHENON, END ELEVATION
Athens, Greece
April 14, 1961
Pen drawing

above

PARTHENON, OBLIQUE
Athens, Greece
April 14, 1961
Pen drawing

opposite, bottom

ERECHTHEUM
Athens, Greece
Date unknown
Pen drawing

<table>
<tr>
<td>

top

VILLAGE

Mykonos, Greece

April 16, 1961

Pen drawing

</td>
<td>

bottom

CHURCH OF THE

SAINTS ANARGYRI

Mykonos, Greece

April 16, 1961

Pen drawing

</td>
<td>

opposite

CHURCH OF PANAGIA

PARAPORTIANI

Mykonos, Greece

April 17, 1961

Pen drawing

</td>
</tr>
</table>

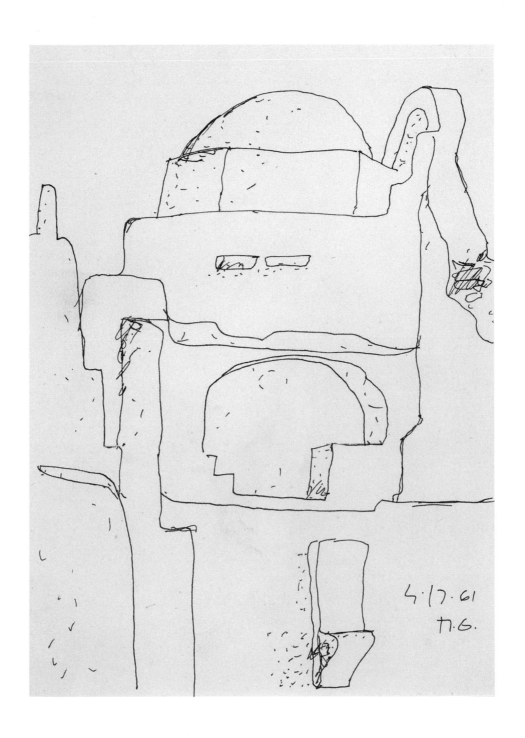

4.17.61
11.G.

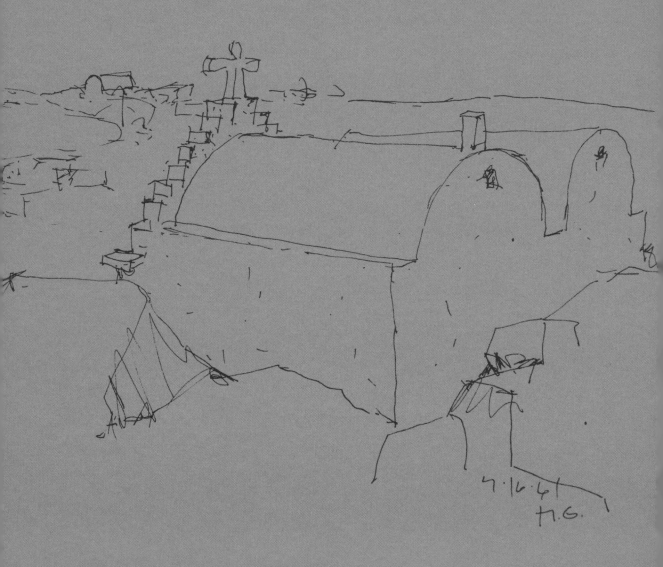

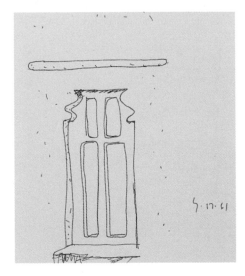

above

CHURCH, SINGLE VAULT
Mykonos, Greece
April 17, 1961
Pen drawing

right

THRESHOLD DETAIL
Mykonos, Greece
April 17, 1961
Pen drawing

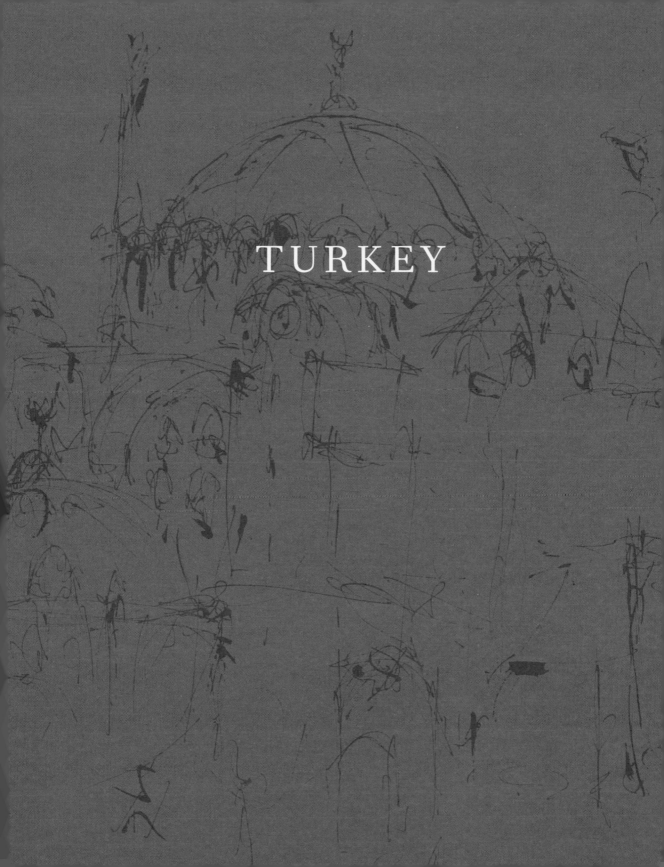

TURKEY

MOSQUE OF SULTAN AHMET I, THE BLUE MOSQUE, NO. 2
Istanbul, Turkey
Date unknown
Pen drawing

"SULTAN AHMET FOUNTAIN, ISTANBUL"

Istanbul, Turkey

1961

Pencil sketch

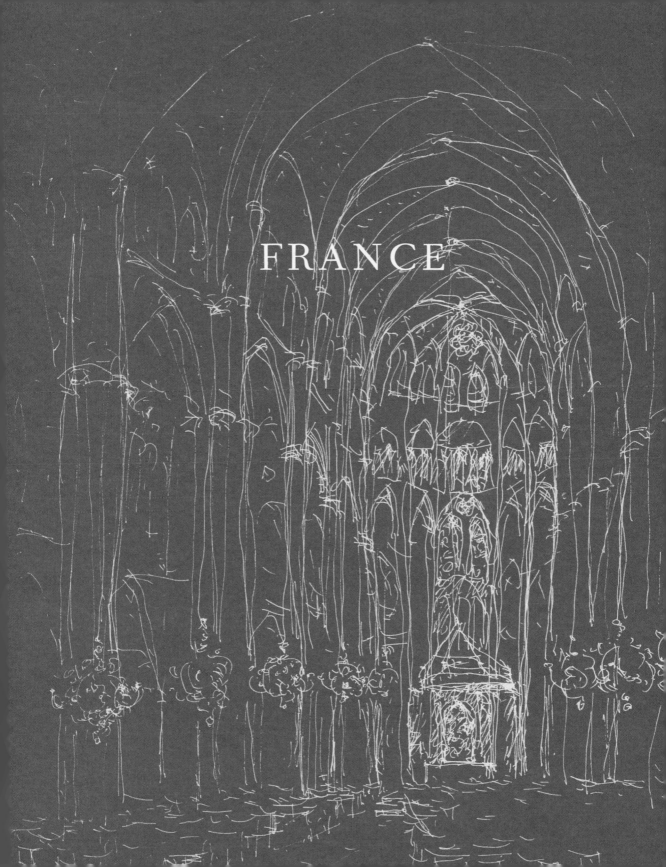

FRANCE

above left

"LE THORONET, FRANCE"
Var, France
September 16, 1961
Pen drawing

above right, left, and opposite

"LE THORONET," NOS. 1–3
Var, France
September 16, 1961
Pencil sketch

"DOLMEN MONUMENT," NOS. 1 AND 2
South of France
September 24, 1961
Pencil sketch

"ALBI," NO. I
Albi, France
September 27, 1961
Pencil sketch

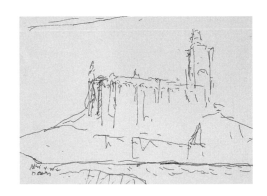

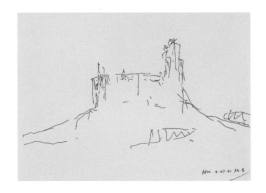

opposite and top left

"ALBI," NOS. 2–3
Albi, France
September 27, 1961
Pencil sketch

clockwise from top right

"ALBI," NOS. 4–8
Albi, France
September 27, 1961
Pen drawing

top
"ALBI," NO. 9
Albi, France
September 27, 1961
Pen sketch

bottom
"ALBI," NO. 10
Albi, France
September 27, 1961
Pencil sketch

top
"ALBI," NO. 11
Albi, France
September 27, 1961
Pencil sketch

bottom
"ALBI," NO. 12
Albi, France
September 27, 1961
Pen drawing

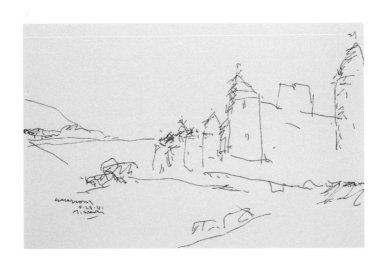

"CARCASSONNE," NOS. 5 AND 6
Carcassonne, France
September 28, 1961
Pencil sketch

"CARCASSONNE," NO. 7
Carcassonne, France
September 28, 1961
Pen drawing

"PONT DU GARD,"
NO. 1
Nimes, France
October 1961
Pencil sketch

"PONT DU GARD," NO. 2
Nimes, France
October 17, 1961
Pencil sketch

"ROMAN AMPHITHEATER, ARLES"
Arles, France
October 18, 1961
Pencil sketch

NOTRE-DAME
Paris, France
Date unknown
Pen drawing

"NATIONAL LIBRARY, PARIS," NOS. 1 AND 2
Paris, France
May 19, 1962
Pencil sketch

"SWISS PAVILION, PARIS"
Paris, France
May 21, 1962
Pencil sketch

"LC'S OWN HOUSE, PARIS"
Paris, France
June 17, 1962
Pencil sketch

"CONVENT DE LA TOURETTE," NOS. 1 AND 2
Eveux-sur-l'Arbresle, France
September 17, 1961
Pencil sketch

"CONVENT, LA TOURETTE,
NEAR LYON"
Eveux-sur-l'Arbresle, France
September 16, 1961
Pencil sketch

"MARSEILLE," NOS. 1 AND 2

Marseille, France

September 17, 1961

Pencil sketch

Marseille. 9.17.61 M. Graves

right

"JAOUL HOUSE, PARIS"
Neuilly-sur-Seine, France
May 23, 1962
Pencil sketch

below

"JAOUL HOUSE"
Neuilly-sur-Seine, France
May 23, 1962
Pencil sketch

above

"RONCHAMP," NO. 1

Ronchamp, France

1962

Pen and ink drawing

opposite

"RONCHAMP,"

NOS. 2 AND 3

Ronchamp, France

October 5, 1962

Pencil sketch

"SAGRADA FAMILIA,
BARCELONA, FROM
THE MODEL," NO. 1
Barcelona, Spain
October 2, 1961
Pencil sketch

SPAIN

Sagrada Família,
Barcelona,
from the air
1926, M. Graves

"SAGRADA FAMILIA, BARCELONA"

Barcelona, Spain
October 3, 1961
Pencil sketch

top	bottom
"SAGRADA FAMILIA, BARCELONA, FROM THE MODEL," NO. 2	"SAGRADA FAMILIA, TRANSEPT OF THE PASSION FROM THE MODEL"
Barcelona, Spain	*Barcelona, Spain*
October 2, 1961	*October 2, 1961*
Pencil sketch	*Pencil sketch*

left

"SAGRADA FAMILIA,
BARCELONA"
Barcelona, Spain
October 3, 1961
Pencil sketch

below

"SCHOOL OF THE SAGRADA
FAMILIA CHURCH"
Barcelona, Spain
October 2, 1961
Pencil sketch

"CASA MILÁ"
Barcelona, Spain
October 1, 1961
Pen drawing

"ROOF OF THE CASA MILÁ, BARCELONA"
Barcelona, Spain
October 2, 1961
Pencil sketch

"CASA MILÁ, BARCELONA"
Barcelona, Spain
October 3, 1961
Pencil sketch

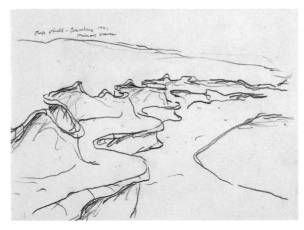

this page
"PARC GÜELL,"
NOS. I AND 2
Barcelona, Spain
October 2, 1961
Pencil sketch

opposite
"PARC GÜELL,
BARCELONA"
Barcelona, Spain
October 2, 1961
Pencil sketch

Park Güell, Barcelona
2.10.4.
M. Craven

Casa Batlló
Barcelona
10.9.61.
Gaudí

opposite

"CASA BATLLÓ, BARCELONA"
Barcelona, Spain
October 3, 1961
Pencil sketch

above

"LES SANTAS MARIAS DE LA MAR"
Barcelona, Spain
October 18, 1961
Pencil sketch

below

"ALHAMBRA," NO. 1
Grenada, Spain
October 8, 1961
Pencil sketch

opposite

"ALHAMBRA," NO. 2
Grenada, Spain
October 8, 1961
Pen drawing

"TOLEDO," NOS. 1–3
Toledo, Spain
October 12, 1961
Pencil sketch

UNITED
KINGDOM

"STONEHENGE," NO. 1
Wiltshire, United Kingdom
June 7, 1962
Pencil sketch

Stonehenge
7 VI '62
Graves

"STONEHENGE," NOS. 2 AND 3
Wiltshire, United Kingdom
June 1962
Pencil sketch

THE NECESSITY FOR DRAWING

TANGIBLE SPECULATION

Michael Graves

IN A RECENT, RATHER TEDIOUS FACULTY MEETING, I made a number of marks on my pad that resembled the beginnings of a plan organization. After making several passes at my drawing, I found that I had reached an impasse. I handed the pad to a colleague who added a corresponding number of marks and returned it to me. The game was on; the pad was passed back and forth, and soon the drawing took on a life of its own, each mark setting up implications for the next. The conversation through drawing relied on a set of principles or conventions commonly held but never made explicit: suggestions of order, distinctions between passage and rest, completion and incompletion. We were careful to make each gesture fragmentary in order to keep the game open to further elaboration. The scale of the drawing was ambiguous, allowing it to read as a room, a building, or a town plan.

After each of us had taken several turns, we realized that the drawing had once again faltered. A third colleague was brought in. He casually dropped in a rather large stair on his first move: the ambiguity was lost. It seemed that, either the game had been so well understood that the jump in scale had reversed the rules, or that the third player had missed the point altogether and his set of marks had subverted the preceding ones. In either case, the speculative aspect of the original drawing could not absorb the shift in meaning that the figure of the stair produced. The game was over.

This little episode illustrates for me something that I previously felt only intuitively. For while it is probably not possible to make a drawing without a conscious intention, the drawing does possess a life of its own, an insistence, a meaning, that is fundamental to its existence. That a certain set of marks on a field can play back into one's mind, and consequently bring forth further elaboration, is the nature of this quite marvelous language. Good drawing, by virtue of this intrinsic reciprocity

This essay was first published in *Architectural Design*, June 1977.

between mind and act, goes beyond simple information, allowing one to fully participate in its significance, its life.

In exploring a thought through drawing, the aspect that is so intriguing to our minds, I suspect, is what might be regarded as the speculative act. Because the drawing as an artifact is generally thought of as somewhat more tentative than other representational devices, it is perhaps a more fragmentary or open notation. It is this very lack of completion or finality that contributes to its speculative nature.

There are of course several types of architectural drawing. By clarifying the dominant nature of each type according to the intention the architect assumes for his drawing, we find three primary categories: 1 the referential sketch, 2 the preparatory study, and 3 the definitive drawing. This sort of classification can never be pure, as all drawings have aspects of each category. However, it is important to identify the primary themes of each.

[1]

1 THE REFERENTIAL SKETCH. This kind of drawing may be thought of as the architect's diary or record of discovery. It is a shorthand reference that is generally fragmentary in nature, and yet has the power to develop into a more fully elaborated composition when remembered and combined with other themes. Like the physical artifact collected or admired as a model holding some symbolic importance, the referential sketch is a metaphorical base that may be used, transformed, or otherwise engaged in a later composition, [1].

I presume that most of us are by nature lazy, and when we see something that interests us in the natural

[2]

[3]

or built landscape, we may deceive ourselves into thinking that we can remember it without drawing. However, if we do draw to remember, the chance that the particular image or set of images will stay with us is obviously increased, [2]. In making such a record of our observation, we of course do so with a point of view. It is that very bias by which the natural phenomenon is interpreted, reseen, that allows the artist to identify with the image and causes it to have special meaning for him. It goes without saying that what the artist or architect chooses to draw, using his sketchbook as a record of observation, reveals the examination of his artistic conscience, [3].

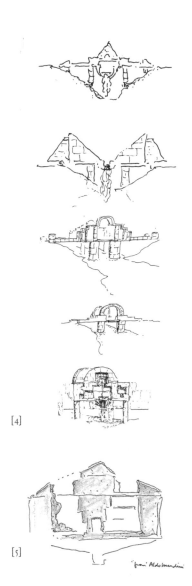

[4]

[5]

from Aldobrandini

2 THE PREPARATORY STUDY. This type of drawing documents the process of inquiry, examining questions raised by a given intention in a manner that provides the basis for later, more definitive work. These drawings are by nature deliberately experimental. They produce variations on themes and are clearly exercises toward more concrete architectural ends. As such they are generally developed in series, a process that is not wholly linear but that involves the reexamination of given questions, [4].

Generally didactic in nature, these studies instruct as much by what is left out as by what is drawn. The manner in which they are able to test ideas and provide the foundation for subsequent development involves a method of leaving questions open through the presumption of incompleteness and the technique of *pentimento*—the erasure and subsequent reconstruction of thematic and figural representation, [5].

It has been said that the modern architect has made but one contribution to the techniques involved in the conceptualization of the building—the use of transparent paper. This medium, capable of being overlaid with successive reworkings of basic themes, may be in part responsible for the conceptual transparencies expressed in some modern building. The accuracy of this assertion is slightly beside the point. However, it is true that the difference between working on opaque and transparent surfaces will ultimately affect the understanding and conceptualization of any composition, [6].

If one regards the plan as the generator of the general architectural scheme, then the initial organizational device, or the *parti*, will derive its clarity and compositional tension from the relative proportions of plan notations, such as distinctions between passage and rest, [7]. As one develops these ideas from general to specific through the overlay of successive plan variations, the configuration becomes more taut through the intelligence of successive decisions, [8]. Further, the plan drawing has the strength to indicate the relative proportions of the vertical dimension in facade and section, [9].

Not all drawings take advantage of this capacity. Compare, for example, the differences between the plan of a building such as the Villa Madama, [10], and Mies's project for a brick villa, [11]. The understanding that the plan notation presumes volumetric control seems to be extant in the former, while missing from the latter.

Though some would have difficulty with the assumption of the plan as the primary organizational device, and would choose an alternate point of departure, such as section, there is still the potential to express the essence of volume in the two-dimensional

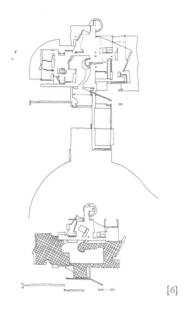

[6]

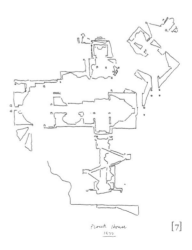

Plank House
1977

[7]

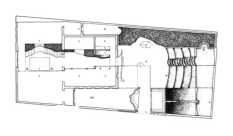

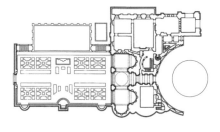

[10]

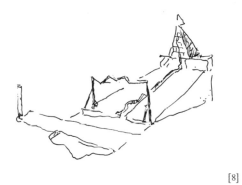

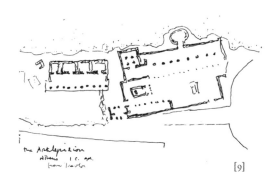

[8]

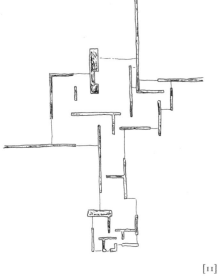

the Asklepieion
Athens I c. AM.
from Travlos

[9]

[11]

drawing. The issue is that the drawing that depicts only two dimensions is capable of conveying the essence of volume and surface—indeed, the aesthetic intent.

3 THE DEFINITIVE DRAWING. This is the drawing that becomes final and quantifiable in terms of its proportion, dimension detail—indeed in its complete compositional configuration. In the two preceding categories of drawing, the burden of experience was placed on the life of the drawing as much as on the architectural conception. In this final classification of drawing, however, the burden of inquiry is now shifted from the drawing to the architecture itself. The drawing becomes an instrument to answer questions rather than to pose them. This is not to say that these drawings attempt to imitate reality; however, they can be regarded as the final step taken in the drawing process that allows the built reality. As in the preceding classifications these drawings must also remain somewhat fragmentary, since no single drawing can explain the several aspects of a building's intentions. The various means of representation of architectural ideas (plans, sections, three-dimensional drawings) show the building as an artifact imagined not so much through the existence of any one of these fragments, but by the understanding of the tension among them, [12].

As an illustration of the three types of drawing, I will refer to selected drawings that were used to develop one of my recent projects, the Crooks House. This was a small house in a rather nondescript midwestern subdivision. The typical suburban solution to the problem of privacy is to locate the building as an isolated object in the approximate center of the site,

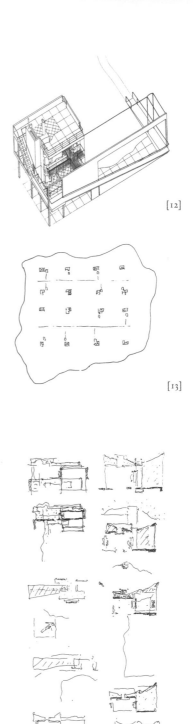

[12]

[13]

[14]

[15]

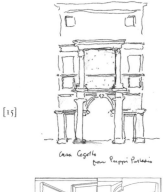

Casa Cogollo
from Puppi Palladio

[16]

[17]

The Annunciation
Botticelli

[18]

thereby leaving the landscape as residue, [13]. The Crooks House attempts to resolve the conflict between privacy and isolation by treating the major formal gestures as incomplete fragments of a larger organization, thereby setting up a dependence between object and landscape. Rather than a single center, a succession of centers is produced both in the building and in the landscape. These centers are linked by their mutual adjustments, which allow them to be understood as a continuum. While the Crooks House is small, it extends its sphere of influence by the fragmentation of both building and landscape, [14]. In this way one attempts to obviate the residual character of the adjoining sites and at the same time produce a spatial continuum that provides for necessary levels of public and private domain.

The referential sketch for the Crooks House arose from my habit of keeping a constant diary of visual notations, a record generally describing physical phenomena that may be employed in later compositions, [15]. A continuing fascination with diptychs, or two panel paintings, has led me to understand that dependencies can be established across a neutral datum, so that the "story" might only be told by crossing that datum, [16]. One assumes that the traditional diptych form inherent in all Annunciations is the ennobling formal gesture that established the conversation or announcement from one side of the composition to the other, [17]. Similar assumptions can be used to enrich the potency of the plan, creating different kinds of dependencies that are perhaps less equitable, but might be seen as more dynamic. For example, the potential of shared centers is developed in Asplund's scheme for the Royal Chancellery, [18].

For me, the idea that seems to distinguish these general themes from others is that I had not only admired them intellectually, but had also made a visual record of them. Because of the act of drawing they were made more accessible to me, for by reinterpretation I was not only understanding the physical phenomenon but also seeing it in my own personal vision. I do not mean to imply that one simply borrows or draws on previously understood phenomena, but it is essential, I think, to bring about an assemblage of ideas appropriate to the fundamental basis of any given work.

In the Crooks House, I knew that the dilemma of establishing enclosure in the open landscape would present obvious difficulties, in contrast to the rather simple enclosing gestures made possible through the physical presence of the building itself. The surfaces necessary to establish those enclosures in the landscape were remembered from the hedge walls of seventeenth- and eighteenth-century Italian and French garden design. This idea of land/building dependency, both in plan and surface, has been a continuing interest of mine, and becomes ever so much more germane when applied to an open landscape with little spatial definition of its own [19].

Previous inquiries into seeing the building as fragmentary or dependent (as in the Benacerraf House addition and the Hanselmann House) were difficult to read because of their extreme level of geometric abstraction, [20]. The preparatory studies for the Crooks House led me to see the relation between building and landscape as less abstract and more figurative. By figurative I mean to suggest that the location of one's body within the successive centers might be

[19]

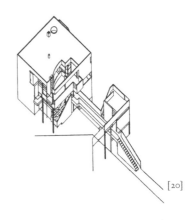

[20]

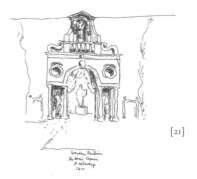

[21]

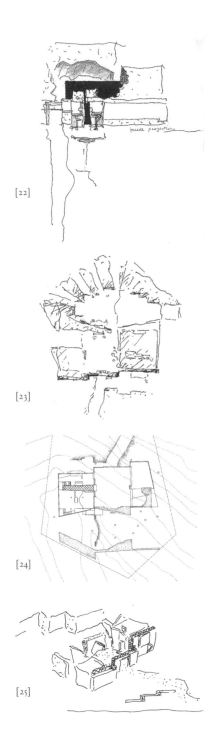

[22]

[23]

[24]

[25]

encouraged not only by plan arrangement but also by surface analogies to both anthropomorphic and natural phenomena. A number of drawings had been made to study those elements of architecture that the classical world regarded as given, but that the modern architect has generally forgotten. The classical tripartite division of vertical surfaces, symbolizing foot, body, and head, was thought to engender a more direct relationship between man and his constructed landscape, [21].

From my initial drawings, which designated gross assumptions of solid and void, figure and ground, [22], one passed rather easily to more detailed notations describing the building/landscape continuity. This continuity was imagined by drawing the land and the ground-level plan as if they were continuous, [23]. The vertical interruptions of surfaces were understood with appropriate thicknesses, ranging from the poché provided by hedge-walls to that of internal service walls. The possible reciprocities of internal and external organization were seen through the similarities in figural notations. I rather literally described the hedge-walls as architectural, and corresponding internal walls as metaphorical hedges. The textural roughness of these analogies was seen in contrast to the smoother surfaces provided by an assumed Cartesian order, [24]. The level of contrast, first conceived of in black and white and further elaborated in color, provided the levels of distinction and continuity that were desired for the building/site dependencies. There was an attempt in these drawings to regard the proportioning of the various plan notations as setting up hierarchies that predicted desired volumetric conditions, [25].

The elevational or surface proportioning in turn played back themes that were initially established in plan. However, it should be stressed that the plan notations were kept "wet" so that both plan and vertical surfaces could remain mutually dependent. Though one started this process with plan notations, the primacy of plan over surface was soon blurred by their subsequent equity in the proposed aesthetic, [26].

Though the plan and elevation studies described the surface proportions, three-dimensional drawings were needed to imagine the building as an insertion in the constructed landscape. The correspondence of plan to the vertical surfaces was tested by seeing the object in the round. The metaphorical analogy of hedge-wall to building wall seen in three dimensions of course reveals aspects of the volume that are restricted by the two-dimensionality of the plan and elevation drawings alone, [27].

The definitive drawings were made to fix as much as possible the various two- and three-dimensional aspects of the entire composition. The rather abstract nature of the line drawings was seen as a method of controlling the proportional aspects of the building, [28]. Where one might expect in the final drawings an attempt to incorporate all the figural and polychromatic interests of the building in an effort to approximate reality, I think the reverse might be true [29–33]. The drawings made in previous stages of the building's development probably come closer to the essence of the imagined composition than the cool, objective renderings of the final drawings. This would seem to leave open and unsaid some aspects of the building's ultimate intentions. However, these aspects can probably be best assessed in the art of both the preceding speculative drawings and the ultimate built reality. In other words, one is still drawing while

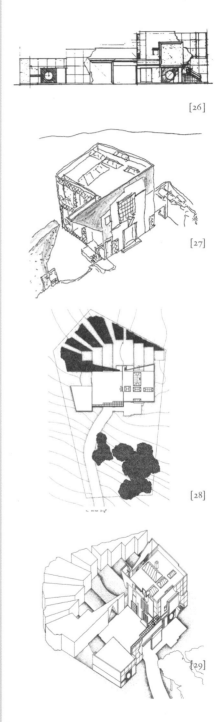

[26]

[27]

[28]

[29]

[30]

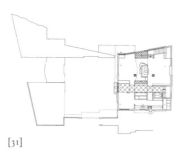

[31]

[32]

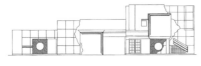

[33]

prescribing aspects of the building, such as its polychromatic value, when the built object can be seen in its context. One is finally rendering the constructed object itself. This approach of course presumes an aesthetic that is open and capable of successive elaborations and compositional variation.

One could ask if it is possible to imagine a building without drawing it. Although there are, I presume, other methods of describing one's architectural ideas, there is little doubt in my mind of the capacity of the drawn image to depict the imagined life of a building. If we are ultimately discussing the quality of architecture that results from a mode of conceptualization, then certainly the level of richness is increased by the component of inquiry derived from the art of drawing itself. Without the discipline of drawing, it would seem difficult to employ in the architecture the imagined life that has been previously recorded and concurrently understood by virtue of the drawn idea.

VOLUME, SURFACE, AND PLAN

AS MICHAEL GRAVES PUT FORTH in his article "Le Corbusier's Drawn References," Le Corbusier described architecture according to three categories: volume, surface, and plan.[1] These elements provide a useful framework through which to look at Graves's own drawings and photographs.

The ability to reduce architecture to its basic forms is a recurring theme in the sketchbooks of Graves and is critical to understanding the development of his later body of work. The sketches produced by Graves tend to focus on the primary volumes of the architecture and strip away any extraneous ornament. This reduction carries over into his architecture, providing an archetypal language of abstracted forms. Graves uses his photographs to capture any detail, color, or texture that his drawings miss; these too become part of his language. Like any language it grows and adapts, but essentially it remains the same.

Graves's twelve drawings of St. Cecile Cathedral in Albi, France (pages 183–187) are the most he produced of any single building on his Grand Tour. Coincidentally, the building also occurs most often in the sketchbooks of Louis Kahn. Graves was fascinated by the history of St. Cecile as a town. As well, he was captivated by its mass and how shadow heightens the purity of its architectural forms. The twelve drawings show the cathedral as a mass that extends from the landscape. In *Albi no. 8* (page 185), the primary volumes in the foreground, the vertical cylinders of the cathedral, and the rectangular spire reduce the architecture to its basic forms. Here Graves consciously eliminates details and concentrates on the presence of light as a modifier of space.

The drawings of Carcassonne (pages 188–191) and the distant view of the Alhambra (page 224) represent similar attempts by Graves to reduce an architectural landscape to its primary mass stripped of ornament. *Baths of Caracalla* (page 76) is an expressive depiction of the space with a minimum use of line work. Its architectural character is revealed through the mere delineation of linear and convex forms. Like

 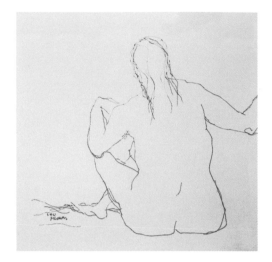

LEFT: *Michael Graves, nude study, February 20, 1961, pencil.*
RIGHT: *Michael Graves, nude study, February 14, 1961, pencil.*

Michael Graves & Associates, El Gouna Golf Hotel and Club, Red Sea, Egypt, 1997–2000.

his architecture, the drawings of Graves break mass down so that varied volumes and an inflected surface might allow viewers to better relate.

In the photographs of Hadrian's Villa at Tivoli (pages 88–90) and the drawing *"Basilica of Maxentius"* (pages 28–29), architectural volume is heightened through the inclusion of shadow. Capturing light, or the absence thereof, as well as the particular quality of light specific to each site is important to how Graves thinks about architecture. For him, shadow is a material that has its own metaphorical potential. He carefully studies shadow throughout his design process, from the referential sketch to the built work. His design for the El Gouna Golf Club and Hotel provides an example. The project's location—the Red Sea in the Egyptian deserts—provided the architect with a blank canvas onto which he could literally paint the landscape with his collection of primary volumes.

These forms recall his sketches of a village in Mykonos, Greece (pages 170–173) and photographs of Ostia, Italy (page 103). Here light plays a critical role as a tool in defining mass as well as serving as an expressive element that can be captured and transformed to varying degrees. Architectural elements such as wooden trellises and deep arcades and windows supplement palm trees scattered throughout the village to provide shade and filtered light and create a natural balance between the architecture and landscape.

Like light, color accentuates form and its relationship to the overall mass. Graves's use of form and color illustrates his dexterity in going between his skills as a painter (the manipulation of two dimensional form) and as an architect (the manipulation of three dimensional form). An ambiguity exists in an architecture that simultaneously implies depth through form, pulling you into the design, and the inverse, when color works to flatten the composition. For Graves, "No matter what the subject or scale, form and color are integrated in one continuous thought."[2]

THE ABILITIES TO IDENTIFY THE BODY in the vertical boundaries between space and surface, and to recognize the horizontal surface of the landscape, on which these elements rest is critical to how Graves thinks about architecture. Through his drawings and photographs he seeks to reestablish the wall as an element that maintains a physical presence as well as a metaphorical one. While in Rome, Graves began to question Modernism's use of the glass plane to create a homogenous world, one in which the outside and inside were visually merged. He wrote, "The long culture of

Georg Friedrich Kersting, Girl
Embroidering, *ca. 1814, oil on*
canvas

architecture that proceeded the modern movement described these two places as different but related. One could frame the quite wonderful light coming into the bedroom, yet could also close that light out to obtain privacy. Those differences, however, began to dissolve with the glass plane."[3]

Graves's sketch of Botticelli's *Annunciation* (page 241, fig. 17) describes the wall's capacity to maintain both a physical and a symbolic presence. In the painting, the archangel in the foreground seemingly places his hand on the frame in the middle ground. This precise alignment implies an impossible spatial condition. Botticelli uses this alignment to draw attention to the division that exists between the interior, the sacred realm of the Virgin Mother, and the exterior of the profane world. A vertical connection is also established by the lily carried by the archangel Gabriel. A symbol associated with the chastity of the Virgin Mother, the flower aligns with the tree in the background and provides an implied heavenly connection. It serves to plainly describe the physical path of the archangel across the threshold.

Georg Friedrich Kersting's painting entitled *Girl Embroidering*, a painting that Graves commonly refers to in his lectures, is arranged in thirds with a frame positioned on each side of the main figure. The frame on the left contains a portrait wrapped in leaves and flowers, while that on the right is a literal window that provides direct and diffused light, creates scale with its divisions, and reflects the flowers on the sill to the inside. The success of the painting lies not in these quantitative measures but in the qualitative effect produced by the light. In describing a candle Graves said, "We enjoy the flame's warmth and its special kind of light. It isn't pragmatically necessary, but socially it's an agreeable thing to do; it's romantic. It's a convention that we have a hard time giving up even though we have other more sophisticated means of warming and illuminating a room. I suppose the reason we haven't given up on the candle is because we'd be missing out on the magic of the experience."[4] Kersting's painting heightens our understanding of the potential of the window as a device that can transcend its physical potential and enter into the realm of the spiritual.

These paintings, referenced often by Graves, comment on the nature of the opening and its physical and, more impressively, its metaphorical role in mediating between interior space and the landscape. His interest in the wall as an architectural element that possesses enormous metaphorical potential in its ability to define the threshold between inside and outside, the sacred and the profane, is found repeatedly in his travel drawings and sketches.

Michael Graves, Entry of Graves Residence, *Princeton, New Jersey, 1991, Ektachrome slide.*

The sketchbooks and photographs show an intense interest in the nature and potential of the wall as a threshold. The drawings of the Pazzi Chapel (page 111–113) are shown in terms of a clear procession and a series of thresholds. They represent the depth of the facade and show an entry that mediates between the scale of the city and that of the human figure. Graves articulates three zones between the profane and open landscape and the sacred interior volume: the threshold defined by the arch, the zone between the arch and the entry, and the door to the chapel. For Graves, this procession to the center of the building is important as an experience within which man can find his own center, thus allowing him to identify with the building. Additional drawings of the Pazzi Chapel take the visitor into the building and show a framed view of the sacristy, another threshold, and the final passage into the carved out area of the altar.

For Graves, the window, too, is an element that provides a clear division between inside and out. His photograph of a window at the American Academy, *Window with Shutters* (page 84), is activated by two shutters, mounted to a stone frame, that are neither entirely open nor closed. The window relates to the scale of the human figure, manipulates the quality of light, and possesses a timeless quality, one described by its aging materials and the ivy that surrounds it.

These same qualities are found repeatedly in the architecture of Graves. The Warehouse, his residence in Princeton, is a guide to how he understands the role of

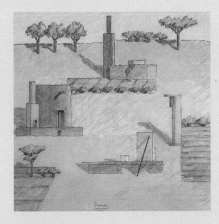

Michael Graves,
Archaic Landscape,
1993, colored pencil.

the wall as a mediator. The entry sequence is a series of thresholds that diminish in scale as one approaches the front door. "Growies," as Graves fondly refers to vines such as wisteria, spill from a trellis over the first threshold and are replaced above the door by a constructed lintel. These elements describe a sequence that takes us metaphorically from a natural landscape to a more formal controlled landscape to a man-made environment.

WALKING THROUGH THE STREETS OF ROME was a kind of visceral experience understood through the facades and streets and squares, through the organization and texture of the city. From his study of its two-dimensional plans, he was able to understand the formalist activity of architects like Baldassare Peruzzi, Antonio da Sangallo, Donato Bramante, and Andrea Palladio. In their etchings he saw the effects of various light conditions on those plans; he found it extraordinary that they represented choices between one kind of possibility and another.

Like the paintings of Cézanne, Graves's *Archaic Landscape* compositions represent the buildings in the landscape in elevation and do not rely on traditional perspectival methods. Visitors enter the landscape from the bottom of the canvas and work their way up through the composition. This describes an arrangement that, while cubist in its pulsations between foreground and background, still maintains a definite foreground, an accessible middle ground, and a background. This simultaneous reading of horizontal plan and vertical elevation is a device used in the cubist compositions of such painters as Juan Gris, to whom Graves often refers. Graves claims, "I like to consider architecture from the point of view of the still life."[5] Other Graves drawings show a compositional equality or oscillation between the horizontal and the vertical surface that allows for multiple readings. In his drawing *Siena, the Baptistry of the Duomo* (page 116), a path that recesses into the drawing can be read as a pyramidal form in elevation. "In the landscapes I'm experimenting not only with the forms of the building fragments as ideas, but also that which is held between them. The idea of making buildings relate to each other in a grouping that is only semi-tight or semi-loose fascinates me. It's probably landscape-related: about the experience of leaving one building and going to another, occupying the ground as well as the building."[6]

For Graves, the plan is a tool for organizing space along the horizontal landscape. In his architecture, he uses the plan to connect a series of experiential vertical planes that define as well as frame space. Such layered series of elevations that can be understood as prosceniums is a common element in his architecture. The photograph *San Marco, Framed View from Piazza Arcade* (page 126), shows a foreground in deep shadow. Where we would expect to see severe perspective in the foreground, the surface in shadow becomes a flattened proscenium through which to view the rest of the image.

The photographs and drawings of Michael Graves are an investigation of volume, surface, and plan. These images reveal elements of an architectural language that transcend issues of style to discover an underlying meaning.

1. Michael Graves "Le Corbusier's Drawn References," in *Le Corbusier: Selected Drawings*, (London: Academy Editions, 1981), 8–25.

2. Alex Buck and Matthias Vogt, editors. *Michael Graves: Designer Monographs 3* (New York: St. Martin's Press, 1994), 74.

3. Michael Graves, "Somehow with Spirit: Designing Rooms with Character." (lecture, Design Center of the Americas, Ft. Lauderdale, FL, February 1987).

4. Buck, *Michael Graves,* 73.

5. Ibid., 71.

6. See Janet Abrams, "Graves's Travels: Giants and Dwarfs," *Michael Graves: Buildings and Projects 1990–1994,* Karen Nichols, Lisa Burke and Patrick Burke, eds. (New York: Rizzoli, 1995), 6–11.

BIOGRAPHY

MICHAEL GRAVES was born in Indianapolis, Indiana in 1934. He received his architectural education at the University of Cincinnati and Harvard University. In 1960, he was awarded the prestigious Rome Prize and studied for two years at the American Academy in Rome. His years in Rome marked the beginning of a long-term relationship with the Academy: he has served there as architect in residence, president of the Society of Fellows, and trustee, and has received the academy's 1996 Centennial Prize.

Upon returning from Rome in 1962, Graves established himself in Princeton, New Jersey as both professor and practicing architect, becoming both an influential theorist as well as a diversified and prolific designer. He is the Robert Schirmer Professor of Architecture, Emeritus, at Princeton University, where he taught for almost forty years. As a young architect, Graves was a member of the so-called "New York Five," characterized as "white" modernist architects of the 1960s. In the following decades, he emerged as a leading figure of an American movement interested in transforming the abstractions of modernism into more contextual responses.

Influenced by his studies in Rome, Graves has continually embraced the idea of designing the complete environment and developed a professional practice encompassing planning, architecture, interior design, product design, and graphic design. The architectural practice, Michael Graves & Associates (MGA) has undertaken a wide variety of projects for public and private clients worldwide, including mixed-use developments, office buildings, courthouses, embassies, museums, theaters, libraries, healthcare facilities, university buildings, sports and entertainment facilities, restaurants and retail stores, hotels, apartment buildings, and private residences. Among his most well-known projects are the Humana Building, cited by *Time* magazine as one of "the 10 best buildings of the decade [1980s]"; the San Juan Capistrano Public Library; the Emory University Museum in Atlanta; The Newark Museum; various projects for the Walt Disney Company; the Denver Central

Library; the Ministry of Health, Welfare and Sport in The Hague; the U.S. Courthouse in Washington, D.C.; and the scaffolding for the 1999–2000 restoration of the Washington Monument. In addition to designing the interiors of all of its projects, the firm has developed an award-winning stand-alone interior design practice. MGA's sister company, Michael Graves Design Group, has produced a wide range of furnishings and artifacts, from furniture, lighting fixtures, and hardware, to housewares and decorative accessories, for retailers such as Target and manufacturers such as Alessi, Steuben, Disney, Dansk, Delta Faucet, Progress Lighting, Baldinger Architectural Lighting, and David Edward Furniture.

Michael Graves has been the recipient of several of the most prestigious architectural awards, including the 2001 Gold Medal of the American Institute of Architects and the 1999 National Medal of Arts, a Presidential Award. In 2005, AIA-New Jersey established the "Michael Graves Lifetime Achievement Award" and conferred it upon Graves in its inaugural year. Considered a distinguished advocate for the arts, Graves has also received the New Jersey Governor's Walt Whitman Award for Creative Achievement, the Arts Person of the Year Award from the New Jersey Center for Visual Arts, the Indiana Arts Award, and the National Sculpture Society's Henry Hering Medal for inclusion of art in architecture. He is a fellow of the American Institute of Architects and a member of the American Academy of Arts and Letters. He has been awarded eleven honorary doctorates. He has lectured on his work throughout the world and has served as a visiting professor at numerous universities. Graves's work has been presented internationally at museums and galleries, and his drawings, models, and paintings are owned by many prominent museums and private collections.

ABOUT THE AUTHOR

BRIAN M. AMBROZIAK studied under Michael Graves at Princeton University and worked for four years as a project designer for Michael Graves & Associates. His own competition and design work has been recognized internationally and has received numerous awards. In 1999, he co-authored *Infinite Perspectives: Two Thousand Years of Three-Dimensional Mapmaking*. He is currently assistant professor at the University of Tennessee's College of Architecture and Design.